THE ADULT'S LEARNING PROJECTS

A Fresh Approach to Theory and Practice in Adult Learning

Allen Tough

Research in Education Series No. 1

The Ontario Institute for Studies in Education

THE ONTARIO INSTITUTE FOR STUDIES IN EDUCATION has three
prime functions: to conduct programs of graduate study in education,
to undertake research in education, and to assist in
the implementation of the findings of educational studies.
The Institute is a college chartered by an Act of the Ontario
Legislature in 1965. It is affiliated with the Universitv of
Toronto for graduate studies purposes.

ISBN 0-7744-0059-5   Printed in Canada

Contents

Experiment with group help for self-planned learning
Reduce the emphasis on credit
Do not rely on a single institution

Preface

During the past seven years, a loosely knit group of researchers in Toronto have conducted several studies of the highly deliberate learning efforts made by men and women. By reporting on and synthesizing these studies, this book provides a broad picture of these learning efforts, which have turned out to be surprisingly common and important.

The findings and implications of the studies, all of which focus on the adult's learning projects, are providing a fresh approach to theory and practice in adult learning. This approach is already proving useful for the researcher and theorist in the fields of adult learning and humanistic psychology. In addition, it provides major implications for the practitioner interested in facilitating the adult's efforts to learn, change, and grow. The book also suggests some implications for youth education in colleges and secondary schools.

My interest in studying the entire range of deliberate adult learning – self-planned learning and private lessons as well as courses and workshops – developed during 1963. During that year, I became strongly interested in several comprehensive questions: what and why adults learn, how they learn, and what help they obtain.

These questions seemed even more important as I reflected on my own previous experiences as a learner and teacher – my years studying psychology and sociology at the University of Toronto; my informal learning as the editor of a college yearbook and while hitchhiking through Europe; my two years as a high school teacher and the surprising contrasts I noticed when teaching my first noncredit adult class; the influence of marriage and a T-group on how I see myself and others; the stimulation of entering a graduate program and of moving to a new city and country. What made some of these learning experiences so fruitful, and others so meaningless? What functions do teachers and other helpers perform in such learning, and what tasks does the learner himself perform?

For my doctoral research at the University of Chicago, I decided to focus my attention on the behavior of adults while planning their own learning projects. With advice and encouragement from Cyril Houle, Philip Jackson, Bruce Joyce, and George Aker, I developed a study focusing on two areas: the teaching tasks that the adult sometimes performs for himself, and the advice and other help he obtains with these tasks from various persons. The study was completed while I was teaching psychology and sociology at the University of Toronto's college of education. As in subsequent studies, I was delighted by the willingness of adults to be interviewed intensively about their learning efforts.

My studies have not relied exclusively on one discipline, or on one school of thought. Although my own background is in psychology and education (especially educational psychology and adult education), I have tried to incorporate insights and approaches from a variety of sources.

Since 1966 I have been in the adult education department of the Ontario Institute for Studies in Education, a department whose members have wide-ranging interests covering many aspects of the learning of men and women. Roby Kidd and other staff members have been helpful in encouraging, broadening, and supporting my studies.

Several studies have been conducted in the department by a loosely knit group interested in the adult's learning projects. This group has concentrated on deliberate efforts to learn in groups and in private lessons, as well as on self-planned learning.

Vida Stanius, a research associate, has been part of the adult learning research team since 1966. Several graduate assistants have spent at least one year on the team, thus contributing much of the thinking and data on which this book is based. They include Heather Knoepfli, Ray Devlin, Stan Searle, Michael Clague, Leonard Shorey, Cressy McCatty, Rosalie Howlett, Jim Fair, Shirley Shipman, and John Morris. In addition, the thesis research projects of Mairi Macdonald, Heather Knoepfli, Cressy McCatty, David Armstrong, Jim Fair, and Larry Denys have made relevant contributions. Students in my courses have supplied additional data and reactions.

Several individuals have also helped me greatly in preparing the manuscript. Portions of the first draft were read critically by David Armstrong, Harold Huston, Roby Kidd, John Morris, Ernest Stabler, Sara Steele, Vida Stanius, Alan Thomas, Anne Tough, and David Tough. In addition, an early plan was discussed with Bill Barnard and Don Blackburn. Editorial assistance was provided by Ellen Choptiany and Myrna Knechtel. Barbara McIntyre and Annemarie Travers transformed thousands of dictated words into a typewritten manuscript, and Barbara McIntyre also performed some of the statistical calculations.

1 Focusing on highly deliberate efforts to learn

Are highly deliberate efforts to learn very common? Why and what do people learn? How much time do they spend at learning? Is their learning self-planned, or do they go to classes and groups? Can we provide better help for individual learners?

During the past few years, these questions have led to several studies with which I have been associated. From the findings of these studies, the following general picture of adult learning emerges.

Almost everyone undertakes at least one or two major learning efforts a year, and some individuals undertake as many as 15 or 20. The median is eight learning projects a year, involving eight distinct areas of knowledge and skill.

A learning project is simply a major, highly deliberate effort to gain certain knowledge and skill (or to change in some other way). Some learning projects are efforts to gain new knowledge, insight, or understanding. Others are attempts to improve one's skill or performance, or to change one's attitudes or emotional reactions. Others involve efforts to change one's overt behavior or to break a habit.

It is common for a man or woman to spend 700 hours a year at learning projects. Some persons spend less than 100 hours, but others spend more than 2000 hours in episodes in which the person's intent to learn or change is clearly his primary motivation.

Many learning projects are initiated for highly practical reasons: to make a good decision, build something, or carry out some task related to one's job, home, family, sport, or hobby. Adult learning is also motivated by curiosity, interest, and enjoyment. A few projects are motivated by credit toward a degree or certificate.

About 70% of all learning projects are planned by the learner himself, who seeks help and subject matter from a variety of acquaintances, experts, and printed resources. Other learning projects rely on a group or instructor, on private lessons, or on some nonhuman resource.

This picture of adult learning has emerged from a series of recent studies, many of which were developed by graduate students and staff members in adult education at the Ontario Institute for Studies in Education. Some members contributed through their own research projects; others played a major role in studies that I initiated.

This book attempts to report and integrate the outcomes of all these efforts. In addition, it incorporates some highly relevant contributions to the field of adult learning made independently by other researchers in the United States, Canada, and the United Kingdom.

THE CENTRAL FOCUS: ALL OF THE ADULT'S LEARNING PROJECTS

In the *Encyclopedia of Educational Research*, Cyril O. Houle (1969) has identified five possible starting points for studying adult learning. One can begin with (1) one or more institutions of adult education; (2) the needs and characteristics of a community or society; (3) the individual learner; (4) a philosophical position; or (5) one or more methods of learning or teaching. An additional starting point could be a body of knowledge and skill to be disseminated to a certain target group.

The starting point of our approach is the adult learner. In particular, we focus on his major efforts to change himself – to learn better ways of doing things, to gain new information and knowledge, to change his perception, behavior, or performance. Our focus includes only highly deliberate learning efforts, not the multitude of phenomena and forces that produce changes in a person without his strong *desire* for learning. Many changes occur in the adult as a result of developmental changes within him, factors beyond his control, his social and physical environment, his casual conversations and television viewing, and his recreational reading. These changes are important to the adult, but they are not the focus of this book. We study only the person's *efforts* to learn: the episodes in which his desire to learn or change is stronger than all his other motivation.

This book encompasses *all* of the adult's learning projects, regardless of what he is trying to learn, why, how, and where. Because we are interested in obtaining a complete picture of the person's total learning effort, we do not restrict our focus to certain methods or places of learning, certain reasons for learning, or certain subject matter.

We do not start, for example, with the notion that learning guided by an instructor or group is somehow better than all other forms of learning. Instead, we have included any learning efforts in which the learner himself does most of the day-to-day planning. We have also included learning that is guided by a set of recordings or printed materials, a correspondence course, or a series of television programs. Learning guided by another person in a one-to-one relationship has also been included, for example, driving lessons, private music lessons, counseling and individul psychotherapy, and some athletic coaching. In addition, of course, we have included classes, conferences, meetings, sensitivity groups, and discussion groups. Some of these may be organized by an adult education agency or extension service, others by a professional association, and others by a service club or church group.

Men and women learn in many ways: by reading books, magazines, and newspapers; by watching television and movies; by seeking subject matter and advice from friends, relatives, neighbors, or fellow workers; by consulting a doctor or lawyer, a salesman or librarian, an extension agent or financial expert. They may also attend discussion groups, lectures, and private lessons.

Sometimes the adult sets out to gain certain knowledge and skill because it will be highly useful in the very near future. At other times he simply wants to possess the knowledge and skill for its own sake, perhaps to have a broad understanding of the world around him. Occasionally the main reason for a learning project is the desire for credit toward some degree or certificate. This book includes all of these reasons for learning and deals with both vocational training and the liberal arts – practical training, and learning for its own sake.

Adults learn a wide range of knowledge and skill. An individual may set out to increase his own self-understanding and self-acceptance, or he may simply want to learn how to refinish a coffee table. He may want to learn about some area of history, philosophy, economics, current affairs, natural science, or social science. He may want to gain more knowledge before making an important decision on the job, or about his own financial affairs. He may learn to play a musical instrument, or to play golf or bridge. He may want to increase his skill in teaching, raising children, supervising, or in some other major task. He may learn in order to plan a trip, buy an appliance, operate a ham radio, deal more effectively with people, or develop a philosophy of life.

Some efforts to learn are relatively brief or superficial. Learning about washing machines in order to buy the best model, for example, hardly seems to involve fundamental changes in personality or behavior. Other learning efforts are aimed at changing one's self-concept, perception and understanding of others, deep feelings, or creativity. Some efforts are aimed at modifying overt behavior, such as a habit, an addiction pattern, or a shoplifting tendency. Some learning projects are primarily cognitive or intellectual, some are aimed primarily at attitudinal and emotional change, some are designed to develop physical skills, and many are a mixture. The term *knowledge and skill* is a convenient way of referring to the entire range of desired changes.

HOW COMMON AND IMPORTANT ARE THESE LEARNING EFFORTS? Highly deliberate efforts to learn take place all around you. The members of your family, your neighbors, colleagues, and acquaintances probably initiate and complete several learning efforts each year, though you may not even be aware of it. When asked about their learning efforts, many of our interviewees recalled none at first, but as the interview proceeded, they recalled several recent efforts to learn. Perhaps

3

this book will open your eyes to some of your own learning efforts, as well as those of your co-workers, your spouse, your students, your colleagues, your political representatives, or your friends.

Highly deliberate learning is a pervasive phenomenon in human life. The 700 hours a year devoted to learning efforts are enormously significant for the adult himself, and for the organization, family, and society in which he works and lives. Although 700 hours constitutes only 10% of an adult's waking time, surely this small percentage affects his life nearly as much as the other 90%. It is during these 700 hours a year, when he sets out to improve his knowledge, skills, perceptions, attitudes, habitual reactions, insight, and perspective, that the adult develops and changes. He resembles an organization that maintains and increases its effectiveness by devoting 10% of its resources to research and development.

Learning projects by members of a society are a means to a better future for that society. When politicians, corporation presidents, and heads of state spend some time learning before making major decisions, their decisions are more likely to be sound. The learning efforts of researchers, journalists, parents, artists, and teachers are clearly important to a society. Several writers have pointed out that adult learning is a crucial factor in achieving peace, reducing poverty and discrimination, increasing the effectiveness of the consumer's decisions, reducing pollution, and reducing population growth.

The individual as well as society benefits from his successful attempts to learn. He gains new abilities and competence, new strength and confidence, an enlarged understanding of the people and environment around him. He can cope better with changes in job, technology, values, and consumer products.

Continuing learning is itself becoming a goal of human life. In advanced nations, more and more men and women are moving beyond material goals, as their lower-order needs such as food are satisfied relatively easily. They are setting a new goal for themselves: self-actualization, the realization of their enormous potential. They are seeking the higher joys of gaining new knowledge and skills, of achieving better self-understanding, of learning to interact more sensitively and honestly with others. The incredible expansion of human growth centers and other means of maximizing human potential is one sign of this shift.

CHILDREN AND ADOLESCENTS Although this book is concerned primarily with adults, we have also interviewed 10-year-olds and 16-year-olds. Their out-of-school learning is extensive, and is similar in some ways to adult learning. Schools and colleges are increasingly recognizing and fostering such learning, thus preparing their students to be competent adult learners.

THE SCOPE OF THE BOOK

One emphasis throughout the book is on the *deciding* and *planning* aspects of learning. The learner first has to decide whether and what to learn (and even why). Then he must decide whether to plan most of the learning episodes himself, or whether to select some individual, group, or other resource to perform that responsibility. If he decides that his learning project should be self-planned, as the majority are, he is then responsible for countless detailed decisions and arrangements. In addition, regardless of who is planning the learning, the learner must decide occasionally whether to stop or continue.

Another theme throughout the book is the *help* that the learner seeks and obtains with the various preparations for learning. Often the help available to him is unsuitable or inadequate. Consequently, several chapters suggest innovative programs and procedures that various agencies or institutions may want to experiment with, in order to provide better help for the adult learner, or to develop his competence in making plans and arrangements for learning.

Related topics such as the following have already been discussed by several authors: the various methods of learning; how to teach adult groups; the social psychological processes in those groups; the structure and administration of adult education institutions and growth centers; the detailed cognitive processes during the learning episodes; the effect of certain variables on the behavioral outcomes of the learning episodes; and psychological development during adulthood. Consequently, this book moves on to tackle some other aspects of the adult's learning efforts. In turn, these insights suggest various implications for theory and practice in adult education (including training and development, the human potential movement, extension, and mass media), library science, self-directed change, schools and colleges, and teacher training.

The approach in this book may also contribute to the new conception of man being developed by certain social scientists, who view man as a self-directing organism with initiative, intentions, choices, freedom, energy, and responsibility. This strongly positive view of man's potential sees him as capable of achieving fundamental and far-reaching changes – in his feelings as well as his cognitive knowledge, in his self-insight and relations with others as well as in his physical skills and aesthetic awareness.

According to this view, at times man is a creature pushed and pulled by his environment and by unconscious forces within, but at other times he can effectively develop plans for changing himself and his environment. At times he changes because of coercion, manipulation, or subtle techniques of control and persuasion by others. At other times, though, he detects and resists those forces, and sets his own directions and goals for change.

2 Episodes and learning projects

A learning project – the central focus of this book – is here defined as a series of related episodes, adding up to at least seven hours. In each episode, more than half of the person's total motivation is to gain and retain certain fairly clear knowledge and skill, or to produce some other lasting change in himself.

For convenience, we have adopted the shorthand label *learning project* to refer to this series of related episodes. "A sustained, highly deliberate effort to learn" or some such phrase might communicate the meaning more clearly at first glance, but seems cumbersome after repeated use.

EPISODES The concept of an episode is the foundation on which the definition of a learning project is constructed. Any one day in a person's life may be crowded with a multitude of activities, and one way of grasping or conceptually organizing this variety of activities is to see how they are divided into episodes. An episode is a period of time devoted to a cluster or sequence of similar or related activities, which are not interrupted much by other activities. Each episode has a definite beginning and ending in time. The activities during an episode include all of the person's experiences (everything he does, thinks, feels, hears, and sees) during that period of time.

A concrete example will illustrate the concept of an episode. If we asked an executive to record his activities between 8:10 A.M. and 9:00 A.M. one day, here are the episodes that he might record: 8:10–8:25 read the morning newspaper; 8:25–9:00 drove to the office. To the person himself, and to anyone watching him, it would be clear just when he was moving from the first episode to the second. This transition would be marked by the executive putting down the newspaper and putting on his coat.

In each episode, the intent or activity remains constant throughout the episode. Other aspects, though, may change. The first episode the executive recorded, for example, was reading the morning newspaper. The goal may change from one article to the next, because one article may be relevant to his job and another may be read primarily for pleasure. But the activity of reading and the place remain constant. In the second episode, the intent (reaching the office) remains constant even though the activities may include starting the car, sitting, and walking, and even though the place changes.

An episode, then, is a well-defined period of time that is held together by the similarity in intent, activity, or place of the thoughts and actions that occur during it. The episode has a definite beginning and ending, and is not interrupted for more than two or three minutes by some other activity or purpose. Many episodes are between 30 and 60 minutes in length, but some are shorter or longer.

The concept of an episode emerged in 1966 in some open-ended interviews about adult learning. In these exploratory interviews, I asked people to tell me about their entire range of learning – about all the different things they learned and all the ways they learned. Most people structured their descriptions in the form of episodes. Each person's daily life seemed to consist of activities divided into various "chunks" of time, each period lasting 20 or 30 minutes, two hours, or somewhere in between.

I became aware that many people plan or describe their day in terms of episodes. In this sense, episodes exist in real life: they are not just arbitrarily and artificially imposed on experience by a researcher. I then asked several individuals to record their activities for a day. They found little difficulty in dividing their day into clear-cut episodes; the time of each transition was clear and precise.

It became evident that focusing on episodes was the most appropriate psychological foundation for defining the phenomenon in which I was interested. For most persons, it was fairly easy to recall and describe an episode accurately, and each episode was clear, definite, almost tangible. Our choice of episodes as an especially meaningful piece of reality has not been shaken by our experience in the countless interviews since then.

VERY DELIBERATE LEARNING EPISODES Now let us narrow our focus. Instead of being concerned with the great variety of episodes in a person's life, let us select one sort of episode – episodes in which more than half of the person's intention is to gain and retain certain definite knowledge and skill. Such episodes can include reading, listening, or watching. They can take place in a library, classroom, store, living room, den, kitchen, hotel meeting room, or train. The person can learn with an instructor, in a group, or alone. The desired knowledge and skill can be simple or complex, deeply personal or almost trivial. The person can use the knowledge and skill for solving a problem, obtaining academic credit, or reflecting on the future of mankind.

Despite their variety, these episodes all have one thing in common: an intent that remains dominant throughout the episode. In each episode, the person's desire to gain and retain certain definite knowledge and skill is dominant. It is stronger than the sum of all his other reasons for beginning and continuing that episode.

We have selected this type of episode, which we will term a *very deliberate learning episode*, or sometimes just a *learning episode*, because it seems especially interesting and significant. These short phrases are a label referring to a phenomenon that is described in greater detail in the following sections.

"Knowledge and skill"

When we state that, in a learning episode, the person's intent is to gain certain "knowledge and skill," we intend the phrase to have the following meaning. The term *knowledge and skill* includes any positive or desired changes or improvement in a person's knowledge, understanding, awareness, comprehension, beliefs, ability to apply, ability to analyze and synthesize, ability to evaluate, judgment, perceptual skills, physical skills, competence or performance, response tendencies, habits, attitudes, emotional reactions, recall, awareness, sensitivity, insight, confidence, patience, and self-control, and/or some other personality characteristic, inner behavior, or overt behavior.

These changes result from experience – from what a person sees, hears, feels, thinks, or does. Changes that are produced by a drug, chemical, surgical operation, implanted electrodes, or illness are not included. Also excluded are attempts to improve one's appearance by adding lipstick or dentures, one's health and energy by getting more sleep or refraining from eating or drinking too much, or one's vision by wearing contact lenses.

It is now evident that the meaning conveyed by the phrase "knowledge and skill" is much broader than the bare dictionary definition of these two nouns. Several other terms might have been equally appropriate: learning outcomes, psychological changes, changes in the person, changed behavior. The meaning we have assigned to the term knowledge and skill is similar to the learning theorists' definition of learning. See, for example, Hilgard and Bower (1966, pp. 2-6).

In deciding whether a given episode is a learning episode, we ignore several characteristics of the person's desired changes. They may be large or small, superficial or deep, useful to the individual or harmful, useful to society or useless, intended to last for two days or for a lifetime. Sometimes, at one extreme, a person tries to produce deep and far-reaching changes in himself, as in learning to deal with a major responsibility such as child-raising or a new job. Or learning episodes may involve a broad and fundamental area of competence, such as becoming more effective with other people. At the other extreme, the purpose of certain learning episodes may be to gain relatively simple information or skills that will be useful for only a week or two.

"Fairly clear and definite"

One criterion of a learning episode is that the person is trying to gain certain knowledge and skill "that is fairly clear and definite." That is, the person must have certain definite desired knowledge and skill clearly in mind. Alternatively, he could be clear on the desired application of that knowledge and skill, or on the question or puzzle to which he is seeking an answer. The desired knowledge and skill in one particular learning episode, for example, might be to understand the structure of galaxies. Or the person may want to memorize certain French vocabulary, or discover a colleague's opinions about a proposed change.

This criterion excludes episodes in which the person wants to learn *something*, but does not have any definite or clear knowledge and skill in mind. Many people attend a museum or a world's fair primarily in order to learn, but have little or no idea of what the content of that learning will be. The decision to take a certain job or to travel may also be motivated by a desire to learn, but with no definite knowledge and skill in mind. The person expects to benefit somehow from such an experience, but does not have a clear picture of just what changes will occur in him.

"Retain"

The definition of a learning episode specifies that the person wants to gain *and retain* certain knowledge and skill. In many learning episodes, the person wants to retain the knowledge and skill for many weeks or years; in others he hopes to retain it for a lifetime. Sometimes, though, the person wants to remember the knowledge or retain the skill for just a few hours or days. Consequently, we have had to set an arbitrary minimum length of time.

The criterion we chose is simply this: the person must want to retain the knowledge and skill until at least two days later. If he is learning the knowledge and skill on a Tuesday, for example, regardless of whether it is eight o'clock in the morning or just before bedtime, he must want to retain it until at least Thursday morning.

This criterion means that efforts to gain certain knowledge and skill for only a brief time are not regarded as learning episodes. For example, reading a set of instructions one step at a time during one's efforts to assemble something is not a learning episode. In that situation the person wants to remember the instructions only during the next hour or two while he completes the next step.

A similar example involves a person's efforts to learn about new washers or new cars in order to decide about making a purchase. This learning and deciding might be crowded into one or two days. If the person was not strongly motivated to retain the information after making the decision, these efforts would not be considered very deliberate learning episodes.

If the purchaser wanted to retain a *portion* of the knowledge for several days, we would have to discover whether the motivation to gain and retain that portion was at least 51% of the total motivation. Similarly, a newspaper reporter might have some slight desire to remember the gist of an incident for some time, but be primarily motivated by the immediate goal of putting the information into today's story.

A salesman learning about a client and his needs before his first and only contact with that client is another example of an effort to gain, but not retain, certain knowledge. That is, the salesman might have no desire to remember the information after seeing the client that evening or the following morning.

Similarly, a secondary school guidance counselor may spend 25 minutes reading the files of the three students he is about to interview, but has no intention of remembering the information past the end of the interviews. This episode seems to be temporary "information processing": it is not prompted by a desire for relatively permanent knowledge.

The reader may wonder why I chose "two days later" or "until the day after tomorrow" as the minimum length of time for which the person must want to retain the desired knowledge and skill. A shorter time simply seemed too short to me. Gaining certain information in order to use it the next day seems quite different from wanting to remember it for a longer period of time. A longer criterion might make as good sense as the one I have chosen. Wanting to retain the knowledge and skill for at least three or four days, for example, or even for one or two weeks, might be an acceptable criterion. I cannot think of any special reason, though, for choosing one of these times instead of two days. In most learning episodes, in fact, the intent is to retain the knowledge and skill for at least a week or two.

It would be possible to establish 48 hours or some other definite number of hours as the minimum criterion. Although this would be easier to understand and communicate, it seems to me that, if the episode occurs on Tuesday evening, there is not really much difference between wanting to retain the knowledge and skill until Thursday morning compared to Thursday evening. However, I do see a fairly important difference between retaining it until Wednesday ("tomorrow") and retaining it until Thursday.

"More than half of the person's motivation"
With notebook in hand, we could follow a person through a normal day. As he begins each new episode, we could ask "For what reasons are you going to perform this activity?" or "What are your goals for the next 30 or 60 minutes?" Our question would be focusing on his immediate reasons for the episode he is just starting, not on his ultimate or long-term goal or purpose.

10

One of his immediate goals for the episode might be to gain and retain certain knowledge and skill that is fairly clear and definite. If this reason is stronger than all of his other reasons put together, we consider the episode a very deliberate learning episode.

Let us suppose, for example, that we are interested in four women, each of whom is taking a speed reading course. One evening, each woman picks up a biography or travel book in her home, reads it through quickly at two seconds per page, and then reads it again at five seconds per page. We cannot tell from the overt behavior of the four women whether this is a very deliberate learning episode or not. Consequently, we ask each woman her reasons for the episode, and we ask her to assign a percentage of her total motivation to each reason.

Let us suppose that we obtain the data shown in Table 1. Reading the book was clearly a very deliberate learning episode for the first two women. By adding together the percentages for the first two reasons offered by the third woman, we realize that it was a learning episode for her, too. For the fourth woman, however, even though learning was the strongest *single* reason, this was not a learning episode.

Table 1 / Reasons for Reading a Particular Book

Reason	First woman	Second woman	Third woman	Fourth woman
To gain and retain the main ideas of the book	0	70	30	0
To produce a relatively permanent increase in the ability to grasp the important ideas of a book at high speeds	90	0	30	40
Pleasure, relaxation, escape	0	30	40	30
Immediate interest in the content (apart from a desire to retain it)	10	0	0	30

The underlying concept may stand out more clearly in Figure 1, which uses a continuum to show the data for the same four women. In this figure, all episodes falling to the right of the 50% point are very deliberate learning episodes. All of the numbers refer to the person's conscious motivation just before the beginning of the episode, or very early in the episode. We are not concerned with the motivation several hours or days before the episode begins.

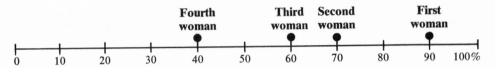

Fig. 1 / A continuum: The portion of a person's total motivation (for beginning and continuing a given episode) that is accounted for by his desire to gain (and to retain until at least two days later) certain fairly clear knowledge and skill.

OUR CENTRAL FOCUS Since our central focus is on the adult's *efforts* to learn, we are interested in episodes in which a certain *intention* (gaining and retaining certain knowledge and skill) accounts for more than half of the person's motivation. These efforts produce a great deal of knowledge, skill, understanding, affective change, and behavioral change in people.

Many other experiences and factors, though, also produce changes in people. Consequently, many researchers define their central focus as any episode or phenomenon that does, in fact, produce some significant change or learning in the person, regardless of the strength of his intent. This is an important and useful focus, but it is not the one chosen for this book.

Instead, for a variety of reasons, we have chosen to focus on the person's highly deliberate *efforts to learn*. In particular, we study his decisions, preparations, reasons for learning, help, problems, and needs.

One reason for our focus is the probability that very deliberate learning efforts account for a large portion of the person's total change over a year. One section in the next chapter speculates on just how large this portion is, compared to the changes produced by episodes in which the person's intent to learn is weaker. A second reason for choosing to study and describe highly deliberate learning efforts is simply that they have been relatively neglected by researchers. The third reason is the most important. The adult's highly deliberate efforts to learn provide an excellent starting point for developing better competence and help in adult learning. A person may be willing to accept help (and accept opportunities for developing his own competence) with something he is *trying* to accomplish. He is not so likely to accept help with something for which his motivation is low.

12

LEARNING PROJECTS In the earlier part of this chapter, we selected very deliberate learning episodes from the ever changing activity of a person's life, and discussed only single episodes. We now use that concept as a foundation for defining our central phenomenon. That central phenomenon – a learning project – is a *series* of clearly related episodes. Instead of focusing on a single episode, we examine several related episodes, usually spread over a period of time.

These episodes may be related by the desired knowledge and skill. For example, the learner may want to learn about various aspects of India. In one episode he reads about the roles and relationships of men and women in India. In another episode he learns about the current economic and political situation from an Indian graduate student. In a third episode he watches a television program describing the life of an Indian child. These three episodes differ in method of learning, in place of learning, and in the particular aspect of the total subject. Yet in the person's mind, they are clearly related by his overall goal of learning about India.

Very deliberate learning episodes can also be related by the use to which the knowledge and skill will be put. A person might undertake a variety of experiences in order to improve his competence as a parent. Another series of episodes might be aimed at obtaining the knowledge and skill necessary for building a boat, solving a problem, or drawing up a set of recommendations.

Time

A series of related learning episodes might add up to a total of 3, 30, or 300 hours. In order to define a learning project precisely, it is necessary to set a minimum length of time. We have chosen a minimum of seven hours, even though most learning projects are much larger than this. In fact, the mean time for a project is more than 100 hours.

There are several reasons for our choice of seven hours as the minimum size. A seven-hour period is equivalent to one working day, which is a significant amount of time to spend at one particular learning effort. In addition, this minimum seems to work out well in actual interviews. We find that this criterion does not eliminate many learning efforts that are especially important. At the same time, most of the learning efforts that do meet this criterion are quite large or significant.

Of course, one could probably argue quite successfully that six hours or ten hours would be just as appropriate a choice. Either of these criteria would eliminate learning efforts that required only two or three hours.

We also wanted to eliminate learning efforts in which the minimum time was spread over a year or two. Consequently, we set another criterion: the minimum of seven hours must occur within a six-month period. The total learning project might

13

last much longer than six months, of course, but we must be able to identify some six-month period in which the individual spent at least seven hours at this learning effort. Otherwise, the effort does not seem intensive enough to include; it seems too diluted or spread out.

Most learning projects go far beyond the minimum criteria we have set. These criteria seem necessary, however, to separate major learning efforts from those that are not very significant or intensive.

Almost all learning projects consist of more than three or four episodes, and these episodes occur on at least two or three different days. Our definition, though, could include an intensive one-day effort that had very few interruptions.

With most learning efforts mentioned in interviews, there is no doubt about whether they fit our definition of a learning project. Our interviewers found that almost all efforts to learn mentioned by the interviewees either met the criteria for a learning project without any doubt, or clearly did not do so. Only a few examples were borderline or doubtful. Some of these difficulties and borderline cases are discussed in Appendix A.

Laymen grasp the concept

Few people actually call their learning projects by that name; many do not even apply the term *learning* to their efforts. They simply regard the series of learning episodes as an interest or hobby, or as part of some responsibility. During the first few minutes of an interview, helping a person to identify his learning projects is often a challenging task. Few adults see their activities related in this way except when taking a course.

Quite quickly, though, the typical interviewee does grasp the phenomenon we are describing and does identify one or more recent learning projects. Indeed, "clearly related" in our definition of a learning project means that the person himself considers the episodes clearly related (by the desired knowledge and skill or by the responsibility or action for which they will be used). The learning project must be clearly defined in his mind, and he must be able to decide without much difficulty whether any given episode in his life is part of the project or not. The learner, not just the interviewer, must perceive that the various episodes are clearly related to one another, and are fairly distinct from all other episodes.

Even though a person may have some professional interest in learning or education, he may have the same difficulty as others in thinking immediately of his recent learning projects. One way to bring examples to mind is to think of subjects or topics in which one is particularly interested, for example, hobbies and other leisure-time activities. Another way is to recall some major problems or decisions

14

that one may have tackled recently. An effort to learn may have accompanied them. One further way to recall examples of one's own learning projects is to think of certain recent activities; reading, television, travel, meetings, or group discussion may have formed part of a recent learning project.

The concept of a *series* of episodes is not just an arbitrary concept that we impose on experience. People do plan and describe many of their activities in this way. Miller, Galanter, and Pribram (1960), for example, have pointed out that people do have plans, and that these plans provide structure to what a person does during the day. When planning a day, the person may have several possible plans in mind, though the details for each have not yet been established. The person then decides which one to execute or continue that day. Although the authors discuss intention in general rather than intention to learn, their concept of plans seems readily applicable to learning efforts.

3 How common and important are learning projects?

The definition of a learning project presented in the previous chapter enables us to tackle the following question: how common and important are these sustained, highly deliberate efforts to learn, change, and grow? This chapter first describes our 1970 survey of learning projects in seven adult populations, and then presents some highlights from several other studies. After discussing people who learn an exceptional amount, the chapter ends with some speculation about the importance of learning projects compared to all other sorts of learning.

THE 1970 SURVEY By 1970, several persons in the adult education department at the Ontario Institute for Studies in Education had intensively interviewed more than 200 men and women on a variety of questions, for several different research projects. Throughout all of the interviews, however, we were impressed by how enthusiastically and how often people set out to learn. As a result, in 1970, we decided to focus our attention more precisely on determining how common and important learning projects are.

We did not have enough interviewers or time to cover more than 60 or 70 persons. To spread our resources further, we decided to select small but careful samples from seven populations: blue-collar factory workers, women and men in jobs at the lower end of the white-collar scale, beginning elementary school teachers, municipal politicians, social science professors, and upper-middle-class women with preschool children.

Several individuals helped with the planning of this study and the development of the interview schedule: Jim Fair, Shirley Shipman, Vida Stanius, Cressy McCatty, and David Armstrong. The first three conducted the interviews.

The interviews were intensive and highly structured. Several probing questions and two handout sheets were developed to help people recall their learning efforts, because some self-planned learning efforts are especially hard to recall six or eleven months later. Few previous studies have probed adequately for them. The interviewers used the definition of a learning project outlined in the previous chapter, and were urged to omit any borderline learning efforts. The interview schedule was revised three times. A copy of the final version is available from the OISE Department of Adult Education.

Quantitative findings

First let us get an overview of the findings by combining the data from all seven populations. Then, after looking at some general impressions, we will examine the details of each group.

The typical person conducts about eight learning projects in one year. More precisely, the mean is 8.3 and the median is 8. All but one of the 66 interviewees had conducted at least one learning project in the past year, which produces an astounding "participation rate" of 98%. The detailed data are presented in Table 2.

Table 2 / How Many Learning Projects Does an Adult Conduct in One Year?

Number of projects	Number of persons	Number of projects	Number of persons	Number of projects	Number of persons
0	1	7	6	14	1
1	1	8	6	15	2
2	1	9	9	16	3
3	4	10	4	17	0
4	7	11	3	18	1
5	4	12	3	19	0
6	7	13	1	20	2

These figures are higher than the figures in other surveys of adult learning and adult education. Several factors account for the differences. Our study used extensive probing by interviewers who were thoroughly familiar with the study's purposes and definitions; as a result, they were more successful than other studies at helping people recall self-planned learning efforts. Also, they interviewed the learner himself, not someone else in his household. In addition, our definition of a learning project differs somewhat from the phenomenon on which certain studies have focused. Finally, the seven populations we chose do not provide an unbiased sample of all adults.

To determine how much time people spend at their learning projects, we used a detailed instruction sheet and asked each person to consider carefully just how many hours he had spent at each of his learning projects. By adding together the hours for all of his projects, we obtained the total time the individual devoted to learning during the previous year. The mean of these individual totals was 816 and the median was 687. In short, the average or typical interviewee spent about 700 or 800 hours a year at his learning projects, though the range was very large, from 0 to 2509 hours. Additional details are shown in Table 3.

Table 3 / How Many Hours Do Adults Spend at Learning Projects in One Year?

Number of hours	Number of persons	Number of hours	Number of persons	Number of hours	Number of persons
0–99	7	900–999	5	1800–1899	1
100–199	3	1000–1099	2	1900–1999	0
200–299	6	1100–1199	3	2000–2099	0
300–399	6	1200–1299	0	2100–2199	0
400–499	5	1300–1399	2	2200–2299	1
500–599	3	1400–1499	2	2300–2399	1
600–699	4	1500–1599	1	2400–2499	2
700–799	6	1600–1699	0	2500–2599	1
800–899	2	1700–1799	3		

We were also interested in the length of the typical project. For each person, we calculated the mean number of hours (during the past year) per learning project. If a person had spent 800 hours at 8 projects, for example, his average time per project was 100 hours. The mean of all these individual means was 104, and the median was 81. During a year, then, a representative interviewee spent roughly 90 hours at each of his learning projects.

About two-thirds of all learning projects were still current and active at the time of the interview; only one-third of the projects were completed or dormant. Our data do not include the many hours that would have been spent at some projects during the months after the interview, nor the hours spent more than 12 months before the interview. (Many projects last much longer than 12 months, as found by Tough, 1967.) A study of only *completed* learning projects would probably establish that they are generally much longer than 81 or 104 hours.

Learning for credit
Less than 1% of all the learning projects uncovered by the interviews were undertaken for credit, which included "credit toward some degree or certificate or diploma, . . . toward passing a test or examination, completing an assignment for a course, or producing a thesis, . . . toward some license, or a driving test – or toward

18

some requirement or examination or upgrading related to a job." If the desire for credit was even 30% of the total motivation for the learning project, it was counted as a credit project.

Despite the detailed questions and the subsequent probing, we found that only 0.7% of all the learning projects were for credit. Apparently learning for credit forms only a small portion of all adult learning. One tends to agree with Johnstone and Rivera (1965) who concluded that "in the main, the earning of formal credit is not an important motive in the educational behavior of American adults [p. 68]." At the same time, one must realize that the actual number of adults taking courses for credit (including full-time students who are at least 21 years old) is rather impressive, even though the percentage is not.

Some "soft" data

Many unsolicited statements and actions during interviews that convey enthusiasm and commitment confirm the quantitative data about the importance of learning projects. A strong determination to succeed, and preserverance despite difficulties, also indicate that many learning projects are very important to the person.

People are eager to talk about their learning projects, partly because they rarely have a chance to describe them to an interested listener. On the one hand, trying to improve oneself – to gain new knowledge or become a better person in some way – is certainly an exciting part of one's life. On the other hand, for some reason, people do not usually discuss this topic at parties or the dinner table. This is unfortunate, because such a discussion can reveal a very positive aspect of a person that is not evident during other conversations. Several times, during an exploratory interview with a family member or friend whom I thought I knew very well, I have discovered an attractive but unsuspected side of the person. Sometimes this impressive new aspect is a goal or an interest, sometimes an earnestness or thoughfulness, and sometimes an intelligent, aggressive striving to become a better person.

Comparing populations

Now let us return to the data collected in our 1970 survey in order to compare the various populations. Table 4 compares the middle or average learner in the various groups by using two measures of central tendency. For each measure and group, Table 5 describes the highest and lowest individual.

Over a one-year period, the faculty members in psychology and sociology spent more time at learning than any other group we interviewed. The typical member of this group spent more than 1700 hours at his 11 or 12 learning projects; one spent 2500 hours. This group was a random sample of associate professors chosen from

Table 4 / Comparing Populations: Means and Medians

Population	Total hours at all learning projects	Number of learning projects	Mean number of hours at each learning project
Professors (N = 10)	1491	12.0	117
	1745	11.5	97
Politicians (N = 10)	1189	6.7	190
	908	7.0	135
Lower-white-collar men (N = 10)	907	9.1	111
	827	8.5	114
Factory workers (N = 10)	800	5.5	146
	799	5.5	116
Lower-white-collar women (N = 10)	430	8.2	48
	425	8.5	44
Teachers (N = 6)	395	10.2	42
	371	9.0	43
Mothers (N = 10)	331	7.2	47
	273	6.5	46

Note. – Each cell describes the average or typical learner in the sample. The first figure in each cell is the mean; the figure below it is the median (the "middle" person).

the psychology and sociology departments of three major universities in Ontario.

Politicians were second highest in total hours spent at learning. The typical politician spent about 1000 hours at his 7 learning projects; one spent 2400 hours. This group was composed of full-time elected politicians at the municipal level in two large cities, including the two mayors. All had been in office for more than one year, and their educational level ranged from Grade 8 to a bachelor's degree.

The lower-white-collar men constituted the next highest group in total hours devoted to learning. These men were a random sample from lower-level positions (including a department store salesman, airline passenger agent, and clerk) in large companies. They had been working at least three years, had never attended college, and were earning less than $7000 a year.

The blue-collar factory workers were a random sample from the receiving

Table 5 / Comparing Populations: Ranges

Population	Total hours at all learning projects	Number of learning projects	Mean number of hours at each learning project
Professors	385–2509	6–18	64–209
Politicians	365–2403	4–9	54–464
Lower-white-collar men	452–1494	4–16	49–170
Factory workers	80–2205	1–10	32–433
Lower-white-collar women	30–919	2–15	15–100
Teachers	159–677	5–20	23–62
Mothers	0–1039	0–20	13–115

Note. – Each cell describes the interviewee who was lowest on the given measure, and the interviewee who was highest.

department of a tire and rubber plant. Their jobs did not require a high level of knowledge, training, mental skill, or interpersonal skill. Each man was between 25 and 45 years old, and had not gone beyond Grade 12 in school.

In this survey, the four groups spending the most time at learning were predominantly male. We turn now to the three groups, predominantly or entirely female, that were below average in time spent at learning, though not necessarily in their number of projects.

The group of lower-white-collar women consisted of typists, stenographers, and secretaries in two large companies. They did not have any children, had been working at least two years, and had never attended college. As Table 4 indicates, on the average they conducted eight learning projects, but spent only 430 hours doing so.

Elementary school teachers in one district in their first year of teaching were almost overwhelmed with problems on the job. They conducted a fairly large number of learning projects, but could not find much time for them.

The mothers interviewed were a representative sample of one upper-middle-class neighborhood. During the year before the interview, each woman's primary occupation was that of mother and homemaker. Each mother had at least one young child who was not yet attending school or nursery school.

Some clear differences were evident within each population, as well as between populations. That is, within each population a few individuals were marked by a great deal of learning, and a few by only a relatively small number of projects or hours spent at learning. Our populations were chosen by occupation, social class, age, sex, and educational level. Apparently many other factors also affect how often a person sets out to learn. These influential factors include the individual's past experiences, his current personality or psychological characteristics, the people around him, and certain characteristics of his community and society. Some detailed speculations about these influential factors are presented in Appendix B.

Other populations

Our 1970 interview schedule was used or adapted in four recent unpublished studies. In each one, the findings tend to confirm the general picture presented earlier in this chapter.

Cressy McCatty, in a Ph.D. study that is still in progress, has interviewed 54 men in engineering, medicine, and other professions. Chosen at random from the assessment rolls of a large suburb, these men spent an average of 1240 hours per year at 11.1 learning projects.

Alex Drdul interviewed 12 successful IBM salesmen. They spent a mean of 1113 hours a year (lowest man: 630) at 13 learning projects; the medians were 1013 hours and 12.5 projects. Approximately two-thirds of the learning was job-related.

David Armstrong, in a current Ph.D. project, interviewed 40 men enrolled as full-time students in an academic upgrading program designed to provide sufficient skills for employment. The 40 men were selected by their instructors: 20 of them because they spent a great deal of time at learning, and the other 20 because they spent an average amount. The higher group, during the year before the interview, spent a mean of 1340 hours at class-related learning and another 1121 hours (13.9 projects) at nonschool learning. The lower group spent 1177 hours at school learning, and conducted 3.4 projects (100 hours altogether) at noncredit learning.

Elementary school teachers approaching the end of their first year of teaching are being interviewed by Jim Fair for his Ph.D. study. His data include only learning that is intended primarily to improve the person's professional performance and that occurred during the first seven months of the school year. The 35 teachers he has interviewed spent a mean of 500 hours at 9 projects.

CHILDREN AND ADOLESCENTS In our 1970 survey, to provide an interesting comparison with adults, we interviewed 16-year-old boys and 10-year-old children. The same interviewers and basic interview procedures were used, but a few minor changes were made in the details of the

22

interview schedule. Only out-of-school learning was included; we did not include any learning projects designed to please the teacher or to get credit toward passing the year at school.

The 16-year-old boys who were interviewed were suggested by the interviewer's friends. She asked her friends to suggest acquaintances who were a little more energetic, busy, and active than average 16-year-olds, and who were reasonably well liked by others. In short, she tried to obtain boys who were above average in activity, but normal in other ways.

About half of the 10-year-olds were chosen randomly from the same neighborhood as the group of upper-middle-class mothers. The others were obtained through a lower-middle-class school. There were equal numbers of boys and girls.

The data indicate that the out-of-school learning projects of young learners are fairly similar to adult projects. Indeed, the 16-year-olds conducted more learning projects than most of the adult groups, but spent only 70 hours at the average project. Further details are provided by Tables 6 and 7.

Table 6 / Youth Out-of-School Learning: Means and Medians

Population	Total hours at all learning projects	Number of learning projects	Mean number of hours at each learning project
16-year-olds (N = 10)	609	9.4	66
	680	9.5	72
10-year-olds (N = 10)	139	6.2	23
	113	5.5	18

Note. – Each cell describes the average or typical learner in the sample. The first figure in each cell is the mean; the figure below it is the median (the "middle" person).

Table 7 / Youth Out-of-School Learning: Ranges

Population	Total hours at all learning projects	Number of learning projects	Mean number of hours at each learning project
16-year-olds	140–922	4–14	32–102
10-year-olds	14–432	2–13	7–61

Note. – Each cell describes the interviewee who was lowest on the given measure, and the interviewee who was highest.

Several differences between the learning efforts of 10-year-olds and of adults emerged from the interviews. First, a child learns a far greater variety of knowledge and skill than the adult. This occurs partly because the adult no longer needs to learn anything further on certain topics, and partly because he has become more selective in his areas of interest. The child, in contrast, has a great deal to learn, and has interests that are scattered rather than focused.

Second, most of the child's learning episodes are relatively short. The child asks a few questions or reflects briefly when his interest is aroused by some remark or phenomenon. Or he reads about some topic for 15 minutes, or watches a 30-minute television program. His learning episodes are rarely longer than one hour, except when taking part in some sort of visit or expedition, or perhaps when practicing a sport.

Third, the total number of hours spent at these learning episodes often does not total seven hours over a half-year period. As one interviewer reported, "Many learning efforts are too short in time to fit our definition. Children tend to flit from one interest to another without devoting a great deal of time to any one area."

Fourth, many other episodes result in a great deal of actual knowledge and skill, but the intent to learn is not especially strong. The 10-year-old tends to choose an activity, hobby, or sport because it will be interesting or fun, not consciously because it will produce certain knowledge and skill or help him become a better person. Perhaps he simply does not think often about the future, and has no thought of how he will change during the next few months or years.

Several of these characteristics of the 10-year-olds are also typical of the out-of-school learning of younger children. By the time a person reaches the age of 16, though, some clear changes have occurred. During his hours away from school and homework, the 16-year-old spends far more time at sustained learning efforts than he did at an earlier age. These efforts are marked more clearly and strongly by the intent to learn. Also, he learns more often in order to handle effectively his new responsibilities and the major problems and decisions that are not faced by a 10-year-old. In many ways the 16-year-old is closer to the adult than he is to the 10-year-old. At the same time, though, much of his learning continues to be devoted to athletic skills, musical instruments, and topics of general interest about which he is curious.

Some clues about new roles for school teachers emerged from interviewing the 10-year-olds. Their out-of-school ("noncredit") learning was often influenced by their teachers. Many learning projects, especially for the girls, grew out of an activity or topic at school, or a question or book suggested by the teacher. The interviewer, Jim Fair, has also suggested that schools can help the child develop the wide range of

24

learning skills and the familiarity with various resources that are necessary for effective self-planned learning. It also became evident in the interviews that the human and physical environment, at home and school, has an enormous impact on the 10-year-old's learning.

NEEDED RESEARCH Our 1970 study has provided an estimate of the frequency and importance of learning projects in various populations. Its strengths included a carefully developed interview schedule with sufficient probing, and interviewers who became thoroughly familiar with the background and definitions of the study. The samples were very small, however, and not all of them were chosen on a completely random basis from a large population. Despite the inadequacies of the samples, the data are encouraging enough to indicate that further research could be very valuable.

There is an obvious need for a study of a very large adult population. The ideal would be a large-scale survey using sophisticated sampling techniques to draw a representative sample of the total adult population in several countries. As part of that study, or before it, several smaller populations might be interviewed. In our 1970 study, we did not reach the highest-level corporation president, the top politicians in a country, the unemployed, the functionally illiterate, the criminal, the very old and the very young, and recent immigrants. In addition, we overlooked student radicals, graduates from schools that emphasize various innovations, and 10-year-olds who have never attended school. And our knowledge about the differences between the self-planned, out-of-school learning efforts of children and adults is very primitive.

A researcher with a fresh approach could probably improve the interview schedule used in our study. The interviewers felt several learners were not recalling or revealing all their learning projects, especially their self-planned efforts. We could not think of any other means, however, of stimulating recall or of reducing the person's hesitation to mention a personal, mundane, or offbeat project. Recall might be improved by interviewing the person every three or four months, instead of hoping he can remember an entire 12-month period.

EARLIER STUDIES Several studies during the 1960s, and even earlier, have noted that many adults make highly deliberate efforts to learn. Some of the studies are primarily concerned with adult education programs, others with adult reading.

Adult education programs
Some of the studies of adult education programs have measured the number of adults in various classes and in other programs sponsored by certain institutions, but have

omitted the 70% or so of all highly deliberate adult learning that is self-planned. Although most of these surveys find thousands of adults in educational programs, these numbers constitute a disappointingly small proportion of the total adult population.

Dramatic increases have already occurred, and will continue to occur, in enrollments in organized courses for adults. Moses (1969), who calls this sort of education "the educational periphery," estimates its total enrollment in the United States as 22 million in 1950, 28 million in 1960, and 82 million in 1975. Cohen (1967) provides some interesting estimates of the total "learning force," which is defined as the total number of learners in schools and colleges as well as in the educational periphery. He compared the size of the learning force and of the labor force in the United States, and estimated this ratio at about 83 to 100 in 1940 and 1950. By 1965, the ratio had shifted dramatically to 127 to 100; the learning force was, by 1965, greater than the total labor force. Cohen's projected ratio for 1974 is 159 to 100.

At least three studies have included learning projects that were self-planned as well as those sponsored by adult education institutions. Depending on the procedures and definitions used during the interviews conducted in the different studies, the percentage of the total adult population that had recently conducted a learning project was 25 (Johnstone & Rivera, 1965), 71 (Blackburn, 1968), and 82 (Blackburn, 1967).

Reading
Several American surveys of adult reading point up the widespread use of this method for learning. Parker and Paisley (1966), for example, found that most adults read at least one newspaper each day. They found that 40% spend at least one hour a day doing so, which works out to more than 300 hours a year. Three-quarters of the interviewees mentioned information for practical use as their first reason for reading the newspaper, with only 12% mentioning relaxation or habit.

Magazines turned out to be an important source of knowledge for adults (Smith, 1963). All but 18% of the adults in the Parker and Paisley study read a news or general magazine, a woman's or home magazine, or some other magazine, such as a hobby or travel magazine.

The average executive spends four hours a day reading business reports and correspondence, business magazines, and other business material. He devotes another 10 hours a week to newspapers, newsmagazines, general magazines, and non-business books such as histories and biographies. "All in all," reported Strong (1957), "he spends at least a quarter of his waking hours with eyes glued to the printed – or typewritten – page [p. 60]."

Books, too, are an important source of learning for at least some adults (Campbell & Metzner, 1950; Parker & Paisley, 1966; Porcella, 1964). Some nonfiction books become best sellers even though written in a technical style, and even though originally written for an audience of specialists. Such books include the following: *Secular City*, *Games People Play*, *Human Sexual Inadequacy*, and *Honest to God*. Their popularity suggests that many people are interested in advanced thinking about such fields as social problems, psychology, sex, and theology.

Let us look for a moment at the person who writes the book, not the one who reads it. Some nonfiction writers conduct enormous learning projects in order to write one book. Vance Packard, for example, took four years to write *The Sexual Wilderness*; he talked or corresponded with 400 authorities, traveled to 10 countries and 130 campuses, read thousands of reports, and read many questionnaire responses. Another example is provided by John Pearson. In order to write a book about Ian Fleming, he traveled more than 100,000 miles, interviewed about 150 people, and made an extensive study of Fleming's private papers.

An economist's view
A noted economist, Fritz Machlup, had already written a dozen books when he decided to turn his attention to estimating the production and distribution of knowledge in the United States. The resulting book (Machlup, 1962) is so sweeping and comprehensive in scope that it is almost breathtaking, especially if read through rapidly at one sitting.

After outlining his meaning of "the production of knowledge," Machlup carefully estimated the number of dollars and workers in more than 30 knowledge industries in the United States. He estimated the amounts of money spent on (1) the education of youth and adults in schools and colleges, on the job and in the armed services, in the home, and in the church; (2) basic and applied research and development; (3) newspapers, periodicals, and books; (4) conventions; (5) other media of communication (radio, television, telephone, and so on); (6) a variety of information machines and instruments; and (7) information services provided by lawyers, doctors, engineers, insurance agents, and governments.

The grand total expenditure for the production and distribution of knowledge was a surprisingly high proportion of the Gross National Product, as adjusted by Machlup: about 29%. Moreover, Machlup estimated that expenditures on knowledge production have been increasing rapidly for some time: by 8.8% a year over a short period and by 10.6% a year over an 11-year period. If knowledge production really constitutes 28.7% of the GNP, Machlup argues, then the production of *other* goods and services included in the GNP increased by only 3.7% (or 4.1% over the longer period).

The number of individuals in occupations that produce and transmit knowledge has also been increasing dramatically. In 1959, Machlup calculates, 21,754,000 persons (32% of the civilian labor force) worked in such occupations. That is, an astounding one-third of all persons who worked spent their time producing, transforming, or transmitting knowledge and information rather than producing something else or performing some other service. No doubt the figures today are even larger: Machlup's figures show a consistent increase throughout the past seven decades.

HIGH LEARNERS Some men and women learn to an extraordinary degree. They are the individuals who spend 2,000 hours a year at learning and who complete 15 or 20 different projects in one year. In their lives, learning is a central activity; such individuals are marked by extraordinary growth.

Several social scientists have detected and studied adult populations marked by especially high achievement, learning, or affective growth. Examples include gifted adults who are also high achievers (Terman & Oden, 1947), the self-actualizing adults studied by Maslow (1954), the outstanding creative scientists interviewed by Roe (1953), men and women conspicuously engaged in continuing learning (Houle, 1961), and the fully functioning person (Rogers, 1961). Describing "the beautiful and noble person," Landsman (1969) said that the same kind of person is also sometimes called productive, efficient, self-fulfilled, self-realized, or a super-person. Maslow (1969 b) has added these phrases: the Good Person, the self-evolving person, the responsible-for-himself-and-his-own-evolution person, the fully awakened man, and the fully human person.

These populations are marked by learning, by efforts to achieve their inherent potential, and by curiosity and joie de vivre. Yet, at the same time, these people like their present job, understand and accept their own characteristics, and are not strongly dissatisfied with their present self. They have the confidence and courage to reveal their real self. They have clearly directed interests: they choose their own career and activities and are not pushed by external forces. They have a strong but realistic commitment to some mission in life. They strive to achieve certain major goals, are spurred on rather than blocked by obstacles, and are productive and successful. Their relationship with at least a few people tends to be compassionate, loving, frank, and effective.

What proportion of the total adult population are we talking about? Perhaps it is the top 10% or even 20%. Or perhaps it is only 1% or 5%. Even these estimates

28

may be too high. Let us suppose, as a very low estimate, that only one adult in a thousand is included. That would still be a fairly large number of persons in any one country: about 110,000 in the United States, 35,000 in the United Kingdom, or 11,000 in Canada, for example.

Behavioral scientists will make many important contributions to knowledge as they continue to study these populations of high learners. The members of this group are especially competent, efficient, and successful at learning. They probably set clear action goals, choose appropriate knowledge and skill, plan their learning episodes fairly easily, and learn without undue effort or frustration. These characteristics make them excellent subjects for studies of effective learning. They are the "growing tip" described by Maslow (1969 a). How can more of these persons be produced? How can other adults gain some of their effectiveness and happiness?

COMPARING OTHER SORTS OF LEARNING

In trying to determine how common and important adult learning projects are, we have discussed such factors as number of hours, number of projects per person, amount of money, and proportion of the labor force. One may also approach the question by asking how much of the change in a person occurs through his highly deliberate, sustained efforts to learn, and how much through all the other ways we have just listed.

A small but intensive study in 1966 provided a tentative answer. After listing the most important things they had learned since finishing secondary school, 20 educators listed the most important activities that had produced those changes. More than *half* of all their choices were learning projects (mostly self-planned learning and courses). Clearly, though, much more research is needed before we feel very confident about this answer.

Learning projects may be especially important for certain persons. If a man or woman spends 1,000 hours a year trying to grow in certain ways, these learning projects will probably change him greatly. The person who conducts only one brief learning project a year, however, is probably affected much more by other activities and factors.

Certain sorts of changes may typically occur through learning projects, and other sorts of changes through other activities. In what ways does a person learn about sex and marriage, raising children, human nature, political issues, his job? What develops his appreciation, sensitivity, mental health, concern for others, self-understanding, self-acceptance? A research or theory-building project might aim to produce a two-dimensional chart: various clusters of knowledge, skill, attitudes, and so on would be on one dimension; various sorts of episodes and factors that produce changes would form the other dimension. It would probably become evident that certain sorts of major changes tend to result from certain sorts of episodes.

The following are some of the forces and activities, aside from learning projects, that produce changes in people.

1. Conversations, newspapers, books, periodicals, television, radio, movies, drama, and travel greatly influence the person's information and attitudes. Although these resources and activities are sometimes part of a learning project, they are often motivated by immediate pleasure, habit, sociability, or a desire for relaxation and entertainment.

2. Sometimes a person learns by observing the world around him, even when the *intent* to learn is not as strong as his other motivation – his curiosity or his desire for immediate enjoyment, for example. The world he observes might include a construction project, art display, sports event, zoo, factory, or trade show. More often, though, he learns through alert observation of human behavior and other common events in his everyday environment, and through thoughtful reflection on what he sees and hears.

3. Often the acquired knowledge and skill is a by-product of some task or responsibility. A person's primary or sole motivation might be to successfully finish a home repair project, chair a meeting, or supervise children. In addition, though, these activities may add to his information or skill, or change his attitudes or awareness.

4. Sometimes a person chooses a job, task, or responsibility because he thinks it will produce some desirable changes in him, or will be "a valuable experience." Other choices, too, are sometimes made primarily because of the beneficial changes they will produce: choosing a marriage partner, a group to join, or a neighborhood.

5. Sometimes episodes that no one intended to occur can greatly influence future behavior. After a traffic accident, for example, the driver may alter some aspect of his future driving in order to avoid having another similar accident. After a child has a fall or burn, his parents may change their behavior in order to prevent a recurrence. Embarrassing moments and frightening experiences also affect the person a great deal.

6. A pervasive, sometimes subtle, influence on the person is summed up in the word *environment*. This includes the people with whom he interacts (usually people of the same social class, neighborhood, age, sex, or occupation), the appearance and resources of his city or town, the political climate of his country, the expectations and norms of his society and employer.

7. The person's brain may be influenced directly by a chemical or by electricity. Psychedelic drugs can produce expanded consciousness, and certain sensations

and images. Some experimental chemical compounds may strengthen memory. Electricity transmitted through electrodes implanted in the brain has made shy women flirtatious, and other people happy or talkative. Brain surgery, or the removal of a gland, can also change a person's typical responses or mood.

8. At least some persons receive information through certain means beyond the normal, well-understood channels. Evidence suggests that some especially sensitive persons can see an object in another room, foresee a distant or future event, or communicate with a dead person. A few individuals can perceive the electrochemical force field around another person's body; in this way they can diagnose his medical problem, know his current mood, or evaluate him for a responsible position.

9. Sometimes a major insight comes from the unconscious mind. After intensive disciplined work at some problem, for example, the solution may suddenly jump into the person's mind while he is sleeping or golfing. Dreams also help us work out emotional conflicts and develop new insights.

ALL WAYS OF LEARNING AND CHANGING ARE IMPORTANT

All of these ways of learning, changing, and growing add up to a rapidly changing individual. The changes that occur over a 10-year span in most men and women are enormous. It is clear that the adult can change very quickly in basic characteristics and insights, knowledge, skills, beliefs, and attitudes.

Changes in adults are a necessary part of social change: the major problems of society cannot be solved without certain changes in people. Without an emphasis on helping people to learn or change, how can we move toward peace, economic development, productivity, zero population growth, more effective government, better cities, widespread physical and mental health, satisfactory race relations – and away from poverty, crime, urban problems, and pollution?

The importance to society of adult learning efforts can perhaps best be grasped by imagining what would happen to our society if all learning projects ceased. What would happen to industrial firms, business corporations, and government departments if the executives made all decisions as soon as they were told of a problem or issue, without bothering to learn anything more about it? Suppose new employees, or those recently promoted, did not bother trying to learn how to handle their new responsibilities. What would happen eventually to our health if all medical personnel refused to make any effort to keep up with new drugs, procedures, and knowledge in medicine? Actually, there would not be many new drugs and procedures in medicine; after all, no researchers would be trying to learn. What would eventually happen in our society if no parents read about child care, if no one attended sensitivity training groups, if no one went to counselors and lawyers for help? What if no leader or citizen tried hard to learn about history, philosophy, religion, evolution, alternative futures, social problems, recreational activities, or the arts?

It is also hard to imagine that one could serve usefully in certain occupations without frequent efforts to learn. The medical doctor and college teacher, for example, must continue learning in order to keep abreast of changes in their fields of expertise. Without spending at least a day or two at learning, a journalist could not write a comprehensive article, an actor could not undertake a new part, a lawyer could not handle a complex case, a political leader could not make a difficult decision, a researcher could not plan a new research project.

It is clear, then, that adult learning and change are important to society and to the individual himself. As a result, many fields of practice and research are concerned with understanding or producing changes in men and women. These fields include personality theory, behavior modification, developmental psychology, adult education, humanistic psychology, organization development, communications and mass media, social psychology and attitude change, learning theory, psychotherapy and psychoanalysis, rehabilitation, manager development, counseling, manpower training, and agricultural extension. Realizing the importance of practice and theory in these areas, foundations and governments as well as universities have supported research and development efforts aimed at understanding how to encourage and facilitate certain changes in adults. Such research and development efforts should continue to encompass the entire range of activities that produce changes in the person's knowledge, skills, attitudes, behavior, and awareness.

At the same time, though, it is becoming evident that learning projects have been a relatively neglected area for comprehensive research and development efforts. Learning projects are far more common and important than anyone realized a few years ago. Studies in this area could make a very high contribution if additional researchers and support were found. Focusing on the person's *efforts* to learn may be a highly fruitful line of research or innovation: only when he has the *intent* to learn will the adult seek new sorts of help and resources that might be developed for him.

4 What people learn

Men and women set out to learn a wide range of knowledge and skill. Some of the subject matter sought in learning projects is complex, difficult, advanced, and abstract; some is esoteric, highbrow, or exotic; and other subject matter is simple, routine, even trivial.

The individual may set out to create major changes in his feelings and attitudes, in his cognitive knowledge, or in his physical skills and overt behavior. He may want these changes to last for a lifetime, or only for a few days. When the adult wants to produce major, far-reaching changes in himself, these desired changes will affect his self-concept, confidence, or mental health. Other learning projects may require only short-term and shallow changes, related only to routine or external goals.

In certain learning projects, the adult merely seeks some specific information that can be used as is. At other times, he must integrate or transform the information before applying it. Most learning projects seek established knowledge, which is gained directly or indirectly from other people who already possess it; a research scientist, though, may set out to gain some original knowledge or insight.

Preparing for an occupation, and then keeping up
A great many learning projects are related to the person's job or occupation. Because performance and attitudes on the job are of great importance to the economy of any nation, this type of learning is very significant to society.

Before entering a new occupation or job, an individual may have to take many courses or learn in other ways. In order to obtain a promotion or major new responsibility, the person may need to undertake an intensive learning effort. Job-related learning projects will probably continue to be important after the person enters the occupation or obtains a new job. At times, he may maintain or upgrade his competence by gaining general background knowledge or learning new skills. Also, as new knowledge is discovered in his field, and as procedures change, he will have to learn in order to keep up.

The range of trade, business, vocational, and professional subject matter is very wide. The fields of learning include electronics, tool design, blueprint reading,

33

business administration, real estate, finance, salesmanship, accounting, law, agriculture, teaching methods, office management, typing, shorthand, bookkeeping, automobile and television repair, foreman training, practical nursing, welding, data processing, and countless others.

Specific tasks and problems on the job

Attempts to update and upgrade one's knowledge and skill are only a part of job-related learning efforts. Many other learning projects consist of just one step in dealing with an immediate problem, case, or task. The person's goal is to prepare a report, make a decision, solve a problem, handle a case, or complete a short-term project. In order to do so successfully, he may decide to spend a great deal of time learning about certain aspects first.

In this situation, the knowledge and skill are acquired for some immediate and definite use or application. The person is preparing for an immediate task or decision, not for some rather vague situation in the distant future. This sort of learning project is often self-planned, because the desired knowledge and skill is rather unique or because the person wants it immediately.

A politician, senior government employee, or top executive, for example, may be faced with a decision that will have a great impact on many individuals, or on the future of his organization or country. Before making that decision, he may devote many hours to learning about it. Many teachers of youth and adults want to improve their performance as an instructor. In order to do so, the person might set out to learn the content to be taught, learn how to use certain teaching methods, or study the background characteristics of the people he teaches. In addition, the instructor can seek feedback concerning his weaknesses by asking his students and others to react to his teaching, or by watching himself in a videotape recording.

Several other examples of specific job-related learning projects are provided by men and women we have interviewed.

1. A lawyer set out to learn a great deal about air crash law after a client walked into his office and announced that her husband had been killed in a plane accident.
2. A community development worker had to read a great deal about the organization and family patterns of the Indian tribe with which she was working.
3. A senior school administrator traveled a thousand miles and expended much effort to learn about possible solutions for dealing with disadvantaged adolescents in his schools.
4. One learning project for an engineer began when he was asked to design a new type of sturdy tape recorder to measure certain factors in an antisubmarine projectile.

5. Aware that his company might begin its first advertising campaign, an investment dealer offered to learn the knowledge necessary for preparing recommendations concerning media, content, and budget.
6. An especially important learning project for a woman working for a children's aid society began when she was assigned several battered child cases. She had to learn the correct legal procedures and how to understand and help the child and the parents.
7. A nursing educator was a leader in planning a new nursing curriculum. In order to plan an effective program, she learned about the characteristics of nursing duties, and about the curriculum and organization of instruction in other schools of nursing.

Learning for home and personal responsibilities

In many learning projects, the person expects to use the knowledge and skill in managing the home and family rather than on a job. In one year, for example, 1,890,000 Americans made a sustained attempt (with or without an instructor) to learn about sewing or cooking (Johnstone & Rivera, 1965). Adults also learn about furniture, rugs, drapes, and other aspects of decorating and furnishing their home. Before buying a house, car, washing machine, tape recorder, or hobby equipment they may learn about the cost and characteristics of various available items. Men and women also learn about budgets, insurance, the stock market, and investing. Other learning projects may begin just before a wedding, childbirth, or moving to a new neighborhood. Through reading, counseling, discussion, or encounter groups, an adult may try to become more effective in communicating and sharing with his or her mate, in achieving a closer and more joyful relationship, and in handling conflicts.

The characteristics of children and youth are greatly influenced by the competence, attitudes, and goals of today's parents. Fortunately, many parents make an effort to learn about caring for a child's health, about the emotional and social development of children, and about helping them develop into effective adults. Parents also learn about changes in schools and society that will affect their children, and later they learn how to set their adolescent children free.

Before making certain decisions of intense personal importance, some adults set out to learn and think a great deal about such decisions. This may occur when choosing a career, deciding which university and course to enter, considering whether or whom to marry, deciding whether to have an additional child, selecting a place to live, or planning for retirement.

The astounding number of practical, how-to-do-it books purchased in Western countries points up just how common it is for adults to learn for home and personal responsibilities. An American study indicates that Dr. Spock's book on baby and child care has been bought by more than 19,000,000 adults (Hackett, 1967). The third most popular book in the period 1895-1965 was a cookbook, and the fourth an atlas. Another cookbook, and Dale Carnegie's *How to Win Friends and Influence People*, were also among the top ten. The lists provided by Hackett also indicate that adults have used more than one million copies of each of the following: several cookbooks, a bartender's guide, several atlases, several foreign and English dictionaries, books for developing vocabulary, home reference books on certain topics (medicine, home repairs and maintenance, housekeeping, marriage and sex, etiquette, gardening), and several encyclopedias.

Improving some broad area of competence

Sometimes an individual sets out to improve his competence in some broad area. The desired knowledge and skill are fairly definite, but may be applied in several areas of the person's life: in his home and family, while interacting with friends and acquaintances, on his job, and in his voluntary responsibilities in his community or some organization.

The individual, for example, may set out to improve his understanding of groups and individuals. This will enable him to be more effective as a group member or leader and in other interpersonal relationships. As a related or separate project, he may try to increase his understanding and acceptance of his own feelings, reactions, blocks, strengths, and weaknesses. He may try to decrease his defensiveness, increase his self-confidence or creativity, or overcome certain fears. He may attend a T-group or a Dale Carnegie course. The person may also try to work out his own meaning or values or goals in life. These may then be useful in guiding many practical decisions.

There are other areas in which learning projects are undertaken to improve one's competence in a broad area. Many adults work at improving their writing style, speaking ability, and vocabulary. Many learn about health, physical fitness, decreasing tension, dieting, or adjusting to bodily changes. The adult may also set out to become more creative and flexible when diagnosing and solving problems, more efficient in all his responsibilities, more imaginative, or less selfish throughout his life.

Learning for interest or leisure

Many learning projects are related to some hobby or other leisure-time activity. In one year, more than a million American adults took lessons in golf, swimming, bowling, tennis, skiing, sailing, scuba diving, surfing, curling, squash, or some other athletic activity (Johnstone & Rivera, 1965). A very large number learned some decorative art or craft such as ceramics and flower arranging. Others tried to improve their painting, drawing, sketching, or photography. Each year, a large number of adults learn to play a musical instrument, take singing lessons, or take dancing lessons. One of every 4.8 Americans play a musical instrument, "making self-made music second only to reading as the nation's most popular leisure-time activity (*Time*, January 14, 1966, p. 49)." Other adults learn about stereo equipment, stamps, hiking, bridge, or pets. Some adults who plan a trip spend many hours gaining information about where to go and what to see.

Some of these recreational interests will lead the person into whole new worlds that were almost invisible before. His new sport, hobby, or interest may lead him to join certain organizations such as a naturalists' club, an orchid growers' association, or a sailing club. A whole world of expertise, technical terms, magazines and newsletters, meetings, like-minded people, standards of excellence, and competitions may suddenly open up before him.

Curiosity or a question about certain subject matter
Many learning projects begin with a question, a feeling of puzzlement or curiosity, or just a general interest in a certain body of subject matter. Some people, for example, want to understand the physical or geographical world, and do so by learning about various regions and perhaps by traveling. Others study the behavioral or social sciences in order to understand society or human nature. Other common areas of learning are English literature, the physical and biological sciences, political science and politics, current events, and economics.

Persons who want to gain some notion of the likely future of mankind may read about probable trends during the next few decades or centuries. In order to gain some perspective about the future, they may also read about past history, about the evolution of man, and about the origin and structure of the universe. Some people want to work out their own set of religious beliefs or philosophy of life. They may learn about their own religion, other religions, or humanism.

Sometimes a dramatic event will puzzle or upset an adult, and he will then begin a major effort to understand what happened and why. A person who is suddenly asked for a divorce or separation, for example, may set out to understand the behavior and events that led to the other person's feelings.

In France, a survey found that geography and history were relatively frequent topics for study (Dumazedier, 1967). In the United States, approximately 3,500,000 people study the basic teachings of a particular religion, or some other religious or moral topic (Johnstone & Rivera, 1965).

AN EMPHASIS ON USE AND APPLICATION A number of studies in several Western countries have shown that some anticipated use or application of the knowledge and skill is the strongest motivation for the majority of learning projects. Most adults, in most learning projects, are motivated by some fairly immediate problem, task, or decision that demands certain knowledge and skill. In relatively few learning projects is the person interested in mastering an entire body of subject matter.

In the United Kingdom, Robinson (1965) found that most adult learning arises from the personal, practical needs of everyday life, not from some intellectual curiosity about an academic body of knowledge. Most people "do not at some stage decide that they would like to know more about economics or psychology: they are concerned about how much it will cost them to redecorate their homes or why their children behave in the way they do. These interests might well lead them quite far into economics and psychology, but they will start with concerns of a personal kind [p. 181]."

In France, a survey conducted by Dumazedier (1967) also found an emphasis on practical and technical knowledge: "The preferred topics are connected to *utilitarian* preoccupations, answering a need for information about matters affecting daily life [p. 205]."

In Canada, a study of 35 learning projects found that the desire to use or apply the knowledge and skill was the strongest motivation in 71% of the projects and was present in every other project (Tough, 1968). In many learning projects, this reason was even stronger for continuing than for beginning. Apparently some learners, as they proceed with a project, discover some unexpected uses for the knowledge and skill.

Also in Canada, Knoepfli (1971) interviewed 21 women who were responsible for forming 21 autonomous learning groups, and found that each of the women, to at least some extent, was motivated by this reason. The 21 women mentioned a total of 66 specific applications of the acquired knowledge and skill.

An early lecturer in the United States (Channing, 1838) declared that self-education or self-culture is practical. "It proposes, as one of its chief ends, to fit us for action, to make us efficient in whatever we undertake [p. 18]."

Knowles (1967) has pointed out that adults "engage in learning largely in response to pressures they feel from current life problems; their time perspective is one of immediate application. . . . They tend to enter any educational activity in a *problem-centered* [not subject-centered] frame of mind [p. 278]." The practical nature of adult learning has also been pointed out by Love (1953), Johnstone and Rivera (1965), and Parker and Paisley (1966, p. III/22).

Houle (1961) found several goal-oriented learners – people who gain knowledge in order to put it to use in achieving some goal. Sheffield (1964) and Flaherty (1968), using factor analysis, subsequently found two sorts of goal orientations: in one the knowledge and skill are to be used in achieving a personal goal; in the other they are to be used for a societal or community goal.

With children, too, the desire to achieve some action goal may be an especially strong motivation for learning. Holt (1967) has suggested that "if we begin by helping children feel that reading and writing are ways of talking to and reaching other people, we will not have to bribe and bully them into acquiring the skills; they will want them for what they can do with them [p. 112]."

DERIDING ONE TYPE OF SUBJECT MATTER OR MOTIVATION Some people denounce or ridicule one sort of learning or another: they scoff at liberal education because it seems useless to the individual and to society, or they express contempt for vocational education because it is just narrow, practical training.

Many of the scoffers divide all learning into two categories: vocational and liberal, training and education, learning for use and learning for its own sake. They assume that any given learning project or course falls into either one category or the other. They fail to realize that both sorts of reasons are present in the typical learning project (Tough, 1968, section 16). It is rare for an adult to learn exclusively in order to use the knowledge and skill, or exclusively in order to acquire the affective benefits inherent in the knowledge itself.

When discussing preparatory education for an occupation or profession, some persons insist that many liberal courses should be included, and other individuals insist that these are a waste of time. Again, the approach taken by both sides presupposes that a simple dichotomy exists. When one looks more carefully at the various sorts of knowledge and skill that are learned for an occupation, the picture becomes more complex.

In a current master's study, for example, Tom Norton distinguishes several types of objectives in the post-secondary training of technicians. These include: (1) manual skills and the use of tools and machines; (2) the scientific theory and principles on which the specific technology is based; (3) general mathematics and science; (4) clear communication orally and on paper; (5) the contributions and context of the particular technology, and its relationships with management and with other technologies; (6) human relations; (7) political science and economics; and (8) the ability and willingness to continue learning about the occupation.

All of these clusters of knowledge and skill are relevant to a technician's performance. Surely it is absurd to declare that any one of them is unimportant to the individual and society, or lacks dignity and prestige. It also seems absurd to deride all these areas as simply "vocational," thus ignoring the range of knowledge and skill that is included.

It seems clear that people do – and should – learn all sorts of things. Some learning will be broad or shallow or superficial; some will be deep or narrow. Some will be practical, related to the job, or useful in some other area of life; some will result from curiosity, puzzlement, a thirst for knowledge, a seeking after truth. Much learning will combine several of these elements.

THE USEFULNESS OF
LEARNING PROJECTS
IN A CHANGING
SOCIETY

Deliberate learning would be important even if there were no changes in the world surrounding the individual. Rapid changes do occur in that world, of course, but first let us look at certain sorts of learning that would occur even without those societal changes.

Some learning projects are initiated because of certain changes that occur in the individual as he moves through the life cycle. He marries and has children. His interests change with age, and he engages in new sports or leisure activities. As he achieves one goal, he moves on to another. As his savings increase, he buys a house or a new car. He receives a promotion because other people in the company retire or die. He receives new responsibilities on the job as his experience and competence increase. These changes and stages in the person's life, and the learning projects they spark, would occur even in a completely unchanging society.

In addition, though, rapid changes do occur in the world around the individual. These social, economic, political, and technological changes not only make an increase in learning necessary or desirable, but also influence the content of that learning.

Some learning projects are necessary to help the individual to *adjust* to changes in knowledge, processes, technology, values, and social organization. These changes affect him on the job, in the home, and elsewhere. He may have to prepare several times for a new occupation, or at least for new procedures and responsibilities in a single job. In his daily life, he must become familiar with new products, laws, recreational and cultural opportunities, and transportation procedures.

The pace and direction of future change in society will be influenced by the adult's resistance or willingness to change in certain ways as a parent, teacher, worker, or consumer. Changes in society will, in turn, result in people learning certain knowledge and skills that are not common at present.

Some learning projects are designed to *produce* or *direct* certain changes in society, not merely to adjust to them. They are oriented toward the future, toward planning or producing social or other change in an organization, curriculum, city, or region. For example, many learning projects occur throughout the sequence of research, development, invention, innovation, adoption. Planning for community or organizational change is often preceded by careful study.

In fact, any major decision of great public importance may be preceded by an intensive learning project. In this way, the most beneficial courses of action can be determined for achieving peace, controlling population growth, reducing pollution and other problems of urban industrial living, and promoting international development. By studying the possible wide-ranging consequences of various routes to achieve a specified goal, public officials can make the decision within a wider and longer-term context.

FURTHER EXPLORATIONS THAT ARE NEEDED As one reflects on what people learn, the need for several further contributions to theory and practice becomes evident. There are many approaches that can be taken to arrive at an adequate picture of what adults learn.

Developing lists

Because most surveys of adult learning have missed so many learning projects, there is a need for a large-scale survey of what people learn. One task of this survey would be to work out an appropriate way of describing, clustering, or categorizing the diversity of knowledge, skills, attitudes, and affective changes in learning projects.

This survey, or a subsequent one, might include adult populations in many countries. Do people learn different sorts of things in France, Germany, Scandinavia, England, Canada, and the United States? Do people learn quite different knowledge and skills, and for quite different reasons, in developing countries? To what extent do people learn different things in Africa, South America, India, and Southeast Asia?

The survey might also include all ages, even children. It would be interesting to know at what age or stage most people learn each cluster of knowledge and skill. In what ways does a person's language change as he moves through the life cycle?

Instead of studying the actual present learning of adults, an investigator might ask what adults *should* learn. Several lists of what children and adolescents should learn have already been developed; for example, *Cardinal Principles* (1918), Bobbitt (1924), National Education Association of the United States, Educational Policies Commission (1938), Kearney (1953), and French (1957). Perhaps, if it is possible to develop one, a comprehensive list of what adults should learn would also be useful. This list might include things that adults should learn for their own benefit, things they should learn for society's benefit, and things they should learn in 1990 or some other future time. By comparing such a list with the results of the proposed survey of actual learning, the gaps between what adults do and should learn would become evident.

New ways of learning new subject matter

The next 20 years might see the development of new ways of learning new things. Developing new ways of learning subject matter that few people now try to learn is a very exciting prospect – it may turn out to be one of the most significant areas of new practice in adult learning.

The last 20 years have produced some important new additions to the content of adult learning projects. Through group and individual methods, many adults now set out to increase their self-insight, their awareness and sensitivity with other persons, and their interpersonal competence. They learn to "listen to themselves," to free their body and their conversations from certain restrictions and tensions, to take a risk, to be open and congruent. Attempting to learn this sort of knowledge and skill seemed incredible to most people 20 years ago. Great changes in our conception of what people can and should set out to learn have been created by T-groups, the human potential movement, humanistic psychology, and transpersonal psychology.

Perhaps the next 20 years will produce several important additions to what we try to learn. In 1990, when people look back to our conception of what adults can learn, will they be amused by how narrow it is?

It is natural for many things to seem incredible to us. Perhaps it is not really impossible, though, to develop ways and resources for an adult to learn how to relax or go to sleep in 10 minutes anytime, anywhere; how to set and modify his life goals; how to perform his daily tasks with half the effort and tension; how to control his heartbeat and brain waves; how to eliminate any bad habit he chooses; how to deal effectively with his own emotional problems and interpersonal difficulties; how to assume effective control over his own physical health; how to assess political candidates and their speeches and decisions; how to choose the best environment and style for any particular task or activity. Already efforts are being made in some of these directions.

In the future, perhaps it will also be far more common for an adult to set out to become a highly sensitive and joyful spouse or parent; to become a much more competent learner or helper; to gain an accurate feeling for his own place in history and in the universe; to express himself in music, poetry, film, and sculpture; to become competent at planning travel and recreation; to expand his consciousness or develop competence at meditation; to become less selfish or more committed to some mission in life; and to learn how it feels to be a corporation president or an Asian peasant.

One of the greatest challenges for the innovative practitioner is to develop new materials and methods that will increase the amount and ease of learning in these areas.